ISBN 1-85576-018-5

Published by Treehouse Children's Books Ltd 1990

Printed in Spain by Salingraf, S. A. L.

MONSTERS

Words by Richard Powell
Pictures by Alan Snow

TREEHOUSE

When I was little I thought there were monsters in my house . . .

in the bath . . .

in the fridge . . .

under the bed . . .

down the toilet . . .

behind the sofa . . .

in my boots.

But now I'm big, I know that monsters
are *not* real.
But if you still think there are monsters in
your house, here is how to deal with them . . .

Monster under the bed.

Bounce on the bed and say very loudly,
''I love doing this 150 times a day.''
The monster will move out to go and find
a quieter bed to live under.

Monster in the wardrobe.

Put a pair of Dad's old trainers in the bottom of the wardrobe. The terrible smell will drive the monster away.

The refrigerator monster.

This monster loves iced-up refrigerators but he hates warm, soapy water. Help Mum to defrost and clean the fridge. Use plenty of soap and lots of warm water. The monster will soon be gone.

Monster in the washing-machine.

These monsters are easily dealt with.
Ask Mum to turn the machine on . . .
to fast spin.
Nobody will ever see *that* monster again.

Monsters that hide outside windows.

Stand by a window, look up at the sky and say:
''Ooh, I think it will snow.''
The monster will shudder and shiver and hurry away to find a warmer place to stay.

Monster in the dark.

A monster would never go out in the dark. It can't see very well and it would only stub its toes. If you saw that you would laugh . . . and no monster could bear that.

Monster in my food.

This monster lives in food that bubbles
and sizzles and is too hot to eat.
Wait. Let the food cool down.
Then eat it.

The boot monsters.

Before you put your boots on, ALWAYS turn them upside down and shake them hard. Any monsters, worms or creepy crawlies which might have crept in will tumble out . . . and run away.

The bath monster.

If you think you see one, try not to think about it. Cover your eyes and count one, two, three. Open your eyes . . . what do you see?

Monster in the toilet.

If you ALWAYS flush the toilet after you have used it, you will NEVER see one of these. Don't forget to wash your hands.

The green jealousy monster.

''Go on, take it, if you want it,'' whispers the green jealousy monster in your ear.
Don't listen, it will get you into trouble.
Simply say to yourself, ''I don't need that.''

Or you could tickle it.
Or paint it red.
Or both.
But it is easier just to ignore it.

The chimney monster.

This naughty monster lived up our chimney.
It dropped sooty lumps into the fireplace and on to the carpet and made my mum very cross.
We called in the chimney sweep.

The sofa monster.

These monsters are very friendly. If you think there is one in your house, take your juice and biscuit behind the sofa, share them with the monster, and make friends.

The monster-under-the-stairs.

THERE IS NO MONSTER UNDER THE STAIRS.

I have an invisible friend called Tom.
He is a monster.
Just for you he is going to make
himself visible when you turn the page.

So that's where all my socks have gone.